CARRY ME CRYSTALS
CHAKRA CLEARING & ORACLE CARD DECK

Joanie Eisinger channeling the guidance of Yeshua
Elizabeth Jarvis | Peter "The Rock Guy" Jarvis

4880 Lower Valley Road • Atglen, PA 19310

Other Schiffer Books on Related Subjects:

Tarot and the Chakras: Opening New Dimensions to Healers.
Miriam Jacobs. ISBN: 978-0-7643-4663-7

Healing Light and Angel Cards: Working with Your Chakras.
SALEIRE. ISBN: 978-0-7643-4695-8

Inspiring Butterflies: A 27-Day Course of Self Discovery.
Marge Richards and Ginny Zaboronek. ISBN: 978-0-7643-3969-1

Copyright © 2016 by Joanie Eisinger, Elizabeth Jarvis & Peter Jarvis

Library of Congress Control Number: 2015957319

All rights reserved. No part of this work may be reproduced or used in any form or by any means—graphic, electronic, or mechanical, including photocopying or information storage and retrieval systems—without written permission from the publisher.

The scanning, uploading, and distribution of this book or any part thereof via the Internet or via any other means without the permission of the publisher is illegal and punishable by law. Please purchase only authorized editions and do not participate in or encourage the electronic piracy of copyrighted materials.
"Schiffer," "Schiffer Publishing, Ltd. & Design," and the "Design of pen and inkwell" are registered trademarks of Schiffer Publishing, Ltd.

Type set in ITC Avant Garde Gothic Std/Minion Pro

ISBN: 978-0-7643-5008-5
Printed in China
5 4 3 2

Published by Schiffer Publishing, Ltd.
4880 Lower Valley Road
Atglen, PA 19310
Phone: (610) 593-1777; Fax: (610) 593-2002
E-mail: Info@schifferbooks.com

For our complete selection of fine books on this and related subjects,
please visit our website at www.schifferbooks.com. You may also write for a free catalog.

This book may be purchased from the publisher. Please try your bookstore first.

We are always looking for people to write books on new and related subjects.
If you have an idea for a book, please contact us at proposals@schifferbooks.com.

Schiffer Publishing's titles are available at special discounts for bulk purchases for sales promotions or premiums. Special editions, including personalized covers, corporate imprints, and excerpts can be created in large quantities for special needs. For more information, contact the publisher.

Cover photo: Color spectrum of semiprecious gemstones in circle frame, on white background © Miiicha. Courtesy of www.bigstockphoto.com
Aventurine, Bloodstone, Hematite, Kyanite, Ruby, Sapphire Photos by: Claudio Foquina
Chakra Key Card created by: Justin Jarvis
All other photos by: Elizabeth Jarvis

Carry Me Crystals is a registered trademark

This deck is dedicated to
the Ascension of the Planet
and all its inhabitants.

From Yeshua
As channeled by Joanie

I came to Joanie in January 2010 as she put pen to paper with the intention of receiving Divine guidance. My messages have offered her clarity on a myriad of topics. Joanie brings forth my wisdom here regarding intention, crystal consciousness, and chakra clearing.

Acknowledgments
As channeled by Joanie

Thank you, Elizabeth, for hearing my call
and seeing this concept through.
Your captured images move souls.

Thank you, Peter, for your crystals.
I hear them calling me.

Thank you, Joanie, for channeling my words
and feeling each crystal come alive as you scribed.

DISCLAIMER

The material contained herein is for informational purposes only. It is not intended to be construed as use for medical diagnosis or treatment. This information should not take the place of a consultation with a physician or health care professional for medical diagnosis and/or treatment.

The user of the contents herein assumes full responsibility for the appropriate use of this information. It should be understood:

1. No diagnosis is given or can be given
2. There are no attempts to heal or cure any condition or situation
3. This is not a prescription for or treatment of disease. There is no attempt to interfere with medical advice in any way.
4. This is not to be used as a substitute for a health professional or medical doctor. This is not a treatment for medical emergencies.

If you are in great pain or discomfort, you should seek a medical professional for treatment.

Contents

Preface 6	Jade 50
Authors' Message 7	Kyanite 52
Amethyst 8	Labradorite 54
Apache Tears 10	Lapis Lazuli 56
Apophyllite 12	
Aquamarine 14	Malachite 58
Aventurine 16	Obsidian 60
Azurite 18	
	Opal 62
Bloodstone 20	Orange Calcite 64
Blue Lace Agate 22	
	Peridot 66
Carnelian 24	Pink Tourmaline 68
Celestite 26	Pyrite 70
Citrine 28	
Clear Calcite 30	Red Jasper 72
Clear Quartz 32	Rose Quartz 74
	Ruby 76
Diamond 34	
	Sandstone 78
Emerald 36	Sapphire 80
	Selenite 82
Fluorite 38	Silver 84
	Smokey Quartz 86
Galena 40	Sodalite 88
Garnet 42	
Gold 44	Tiger's Eye 90
Granite 46	Topaz 92
	Turquoise 94
Hematite 48	

Preface

These gems are precious. Each one can assist you on your journey to enlightenment. Peace is a goal for some, and happiness, abundance, and Love is for others. In this book I have compiled information so you can enjoy learning about each crystal in a more detailed fashion.

I have included elements, such as Gold and Silver. They brighten your world. Precious commodities assist in shifting your perspective to help you heal.

Carry Me Crystals is a powerful multipurpose deck that can be used in a variety of ways. If a particular crystal resonates with you, please hold it and enjoy the fruits of its energy. If the message on the reverse side of a card speaks to you, you may follow its guidance. Play with picking a card from the deck if you wish to use it as an oracle. Several crystals might speak to you simultaneously; go inside yourself and see what their messages are telling you. —Yeshua, as channeled by Joanie

Each card is coded with a color dot (see color dot key card representing the chakra(s) associated with it. When you intentionally work with a stone to heal a particular chakra, miracles can occur. If you are new to chakra clearing or clearing with cards using intention, be patient and allow yourself to be the student. The crystals' energies will work with you no matter your level of

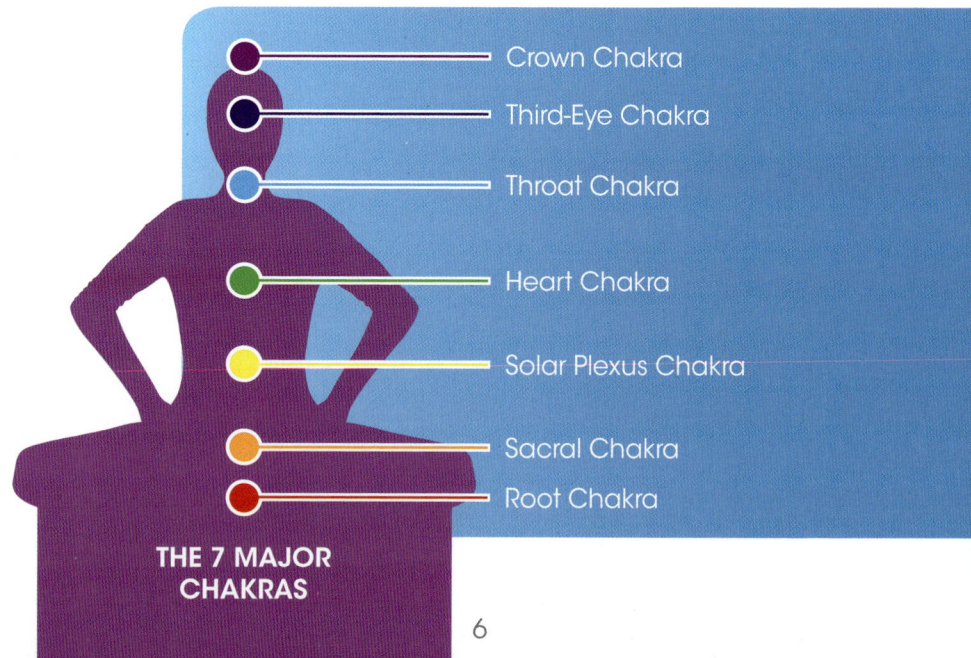

THE 7 MAJOR CHAKRAS

experience or understanding of the work. You may require numerous sessions with a crystal if buried issues are dense or multilayered. Trust your guidance regarding when to return to a particular crystal for further work. Please remember to "clear" your cards before each session by blowing or tapping on them to clear any negative energies they might have attracted.

If you have any questions, or you wish to contact us, you can find us at the below email addresses:

Joanie Eisinger: info@joanieswhitelighthealing.com
Peter Jarvis: pacoman104@gmail.com
Elizabeth Jarvis: awakeninawe@gmail.com

We would love to hear how *Carry Me Crystals* has served you.

Authors' Message

What if you did not have access to a particular crystal and wished to work with it? We believe that the power of intention, the creative use of thoughts and words, can serve to remedy this for you. A crystal's picture and its written name have a frequency equivalent to that of its third dimensional (physical) counterpart. Carrying a crystal card is like carrying the intention, or frequency, of the actual object. In effect, the card opens the intention that the crystal carries. The image pictured on each card represents an aspect, or energetic piece, of the stone's "oversoul" that resides in Creation and is of service to us all. You energize its properties using your belief that you are working with a "living consciousness" and the work begins!

The size of the card is purposely smaller than other card decks because we wish for you to pocket them as you journey each day.

We collectively intend to bring you more than you thought possible. For some, this is a novel concept; for others, old hat. Wherever you are on your journey with using intention, working with crystals, or clearing chakras, we hope you enjoy *Carry Me Crystals*.

Amethyst

- ## "Third-Eye Chakra"

When Amethyst is repeatedly used for third-eye enhancement, it gets tired. The gemstone is used and abused often. Using intention, imagine you are cleansing or "washing" Amethyst by bathing it in gray light. The stone will now be clear. Good. Keep these processes to a minimum as Amethyst wishes balance. In relation to third-eye work, please be gentle with its use. When you place it over this chakra (found in the middle of your forehead), you may feel Light pour in. This creates a wave, or bubble, that cannot be replicated by other stones. Do you see how important it is to use a crystal that creates ripples in Divine sight? I say no stone moves energy in and around the way Amethyst does. Work with intention and be creative. Will you escape trouble, enhance beauty, mine caves? All is possible. The work here is Divine in that you can create movies or images that change time-space reality. Yes, please be careful when you use your third eye for manifesting visions or creations you desire. All concepts hold weight. They are serious and are considered special by angels who see the work you do. When Amethyst is used to create reality wishes, it gets tired. Therefore, please use it sparingly, for about ten minutes. After your work is done, bathe the card in Light. Put the intention there that Love is in the stone to release what needs to be healed so it may work optimally with you again.

- **"Crown Chakra"**

Amethyst is the jewel many wear. She belongs atop a pyramid. Take the gem and place her on top of your head. If you cannot balance the crystal card, use intention to virtually place Amethyst there. Then, imagine Amethyst connecting with fairies, elves—anything Divine. If you sit with Amethyst energy and meditate, you will often see purple, hear ringing, and wish you had better balance because you are transported high to Heaven. This stone can be used as a meditation device in that it transports you to realms that are inspiring and beautiful. Incandescent light makes the gem shine. Please note that some are "allergic" to it. Yes, they are unable to be with it, for they have not mastered issues related to their chakras below the crown. There is a need to be grounded, centered, and unwavering before Amethyst is utilized to its maximum potential.

Apache Tears

- *"Root Chakra"*

This unique blend of minerals is formed in remote locations, distant from many tropical places and lands with oases. The Tear has several properties: there are minerals within that lend to salvation, or freeing pain from lifetimes of loss, slavery, and institutions that committed crimes against tribes. The most precious herb is found in this stone: rosehip. Other herbs are within, yet many cannot access their energies due to their inability to channel crystals. Apache Tears often attracts sad and uncompromising feelings; therefore, you can use sage to clear this crystal. Apache Tears is a light-weighted stone, yet its theme is about sadness, which is heavy-weighted.

In order to clear a stone, one needs to place it on a cloth near sunlight or moonlight. Apache Tears needs plenty of rest. Take it and light it up with the sun or moon for a day. This refreshes the baby. Now, it's ready for work. Can you imagine taking a stone from the window and using it for many purposes? Let's see:

Rose Quartz and Obsidian are friends with this Tear gem. They sit in tandem. If you place each on a bedframe, it can eliminate sad feelings. Try this as you ready yourself for bed.

Now, there are other purposes for our using the Tear. We need you to take time to list problems you have in your life. If you do this, place the Tear on the list. Mention out loud that you wish to release troubles to God, Source—whoever you feel supports and protects your life. Then, take a nap; go to sleep. Dream of the stone carrying you to another dimension that's worry-free.

More work: Apache Tears can magnify your present sadness, so please be mindful to use it when you are happy and hopeful. This is important. The main reason I say this is for your health.

Please know that you are always able to clear painful emotions. It is my wish that you imagine your ability to heal is great. "Simple," you say. "Yes," I reply.

The root chakra needs assistance with respect to clearing out all worries about family, independence, breaking the mold, moving from home, being an independent thinker, having the ability to move to new vistas, and seeing new perspectives. Many themes here center around losing, gaining, retrieving, obtaining, and gearing up the courage to be different from the group.

Call upon the card to assist you when you wish to clear family, religious, and educational issues. The card can be placed over the base of the spine, or you can intend it sits there while you clear the energy around the matter(s) concerning you. When you meditate, you may see this is easy. Cares wash over you and much Love shines through your crown. Come to terms with issues and it will be easier to release this debris—the misconceptions and misunderstandings residing in your root chakra.

It is a good stone, a "heart-y" one that wishes alignment with you. Remember to take care of it and clear it after your work is done.

Apophyllite

- **"Third-Eye Chakra"**

This begins a segment on "eye care." If you pull out the garbage that has accumulated in your life, you will say that the third eye is clogged and permits little Light to shine through. We need Apophyllite to clean the machine called the third eye.

Place the card over your brow, in the middle of your forehead. With little help, the moment you put the card there, the information is put in. Many messages of hope and peace permeate your consciousness so you are able to complete this process. Numerous channels are opened and sad, scary, and worrisome thoughts are removed. You can now imagine problems being released and you are able to see your issues with more clarity. Try to envision a lighter space between your eyes, above your head. If less sadness exists here, more Light can shine in to create a peaceful environment. You will then be able to get in touch with issues concerning future ideas and dreams you wish to create. You can also see how others hurt and see how to remedy situations in an aligned, centered manner. Third eye work involves opening yourself to the possibility that you can be anything if you see or dream it. See the vision. Make it happen. Be alive. See the dream.

• "Crown Chakra"

This "Master Stone" requires ingenuity and finesse. It is practical because it finds a way to work through many situations. It is unable to work if you are tired, so do not bother to work on resolving issues if it's bedtime. This stone can be used for enlightenment. Yes. Enlightenment. If you wish "more," "higher," and "better," consider Apophyllite. To get started, take the card, hold it in your hand, and bless the stone, taking care to wash it (clear it) of any previous worries that were attached to it in past healings and meditations. The stone, now clear, can be put on a shelf for safe keeping. Twenty-four hours later, return to find it ready for work. Go to a quiet place, sit, meditate, or think peacefully about how you wish to Divinely open. If you present your request to the Universe peacefully, the reaction from Apophyllite is peaceful, as well. If you jump into the exercise, it will recoil. So, make sure you are quiet and steady. If you wish to connect with Buddha, ask, in Love, that He be with you. The gem responds in a sparkly manner—lights before your eyes and twinkles in your head. You glow. When I come visit you to assist Apophyllite, I march in quite confidently. We work together very practically. Meditate and connect with Divinity in all ways. Be quiet and proceed slowly with her. Apophyllite teems with joy and only wishes to be treated with care and with softness.

Aquamarine

- ## "Heart Chakra"

When Aquamarine is used to settle Love situations, it speaks quickly. This means it works at a frequency that is sped up so negative vibrations are pulled up and out easily. Use it with caution, for it is powerful. Please take steps to prepare yourself before placing the intention to clear heart issues. First, sit quietly. Examine life situations concerning Love (self-Love and Love for others). Then, pray this action of intentional healing be protected by Archangel Michael. Archangel Uriel attracts energy for healing, placing it near your head so you can blend forces with the crystal. Now, the card is to be handled carefully and prudently. Without knowing anything about the properties of this stone, it is possible to harm yourself. Therefore, trust that the Universe guides you to be safe and takes measures to work swiftly and easily without interruption. I share this with you, for the information clears up many misunderstandings that "a rock is just a rock and no harm can come from playing in the ethers with this."

Heart issues cry out and are released quickly. Work for a few minutes at maximum with Aquamarine. We need prudence. If you see happy visions, stop the work. If you are sad, continue a few minutes more. If sadness persists, I suggest you leave the work and resume the following week.

The heart is ready for release when you feel a glow or warmth from within. If you do not, it is still possible that you are releasing sadness. Become the warrior: Sit quietly and demand the departure of wounds not serving you. The crystal completes the act by pulling out sources of pain. In a few minutes, the work is done. Rest. Praise God, Source, for Its assistance in the process.

It is terrific when you can ultimately heal yourself. With intention and the genuine belief in the process, you can eliminate lifetimes of grief. Your heart thanks you.

- "Throat Chakra"

The piece of information I wish to impart here is important: If you take Aquamarine and sit quietly, singing might occur. I believe it opens the throat, making it very easy to feel joy. How do you do this? Place "Aqua-Mae" on a tissue. Wipe the card on both sides, cleaning off fingerprints and dirt. Then, place it in a hand and meditate. Three minutes is enough. Take the card, place it near your throat, eliminating sad feelings of longing. The tune of Love streams in and many feel Light pour to their throat. Oftentimes, the throat sings to pierce through sadness. It is a mining out, a chipping away of life's dreariness through music—toning that leaves one speechless, yet full of song. Can you work the stone in this manner? It is special in that music makes it sing. Place Aquamarine near the stereo and watch the glow. We think you will enjoy her vibe.

Aventurine (GREEN)

- ## "Heart Chakra"

Hold Aventurine close to your heart (center of chest). Why? Because the necessary course of action involves direct—absolute direct—contact with the chakra of Love. Touch the crystal there. See the Love, feel the Love...It's a precious moment. Yes... Aventurine is a classic stone. It liquefies grief and longing, pushing out unnecessary problems. The goal is to have a light heart that can manage functional relationships very well. ("Functional" means spousal and all other relationships involving communication and intimacy.)

Do you want more Love? If so, put the stone on your heart. Lie down. Imagine—truly believe you have a Love that is Divine and blessed. Envision more than you imagine now. Yes. Just believe you are enhancing the vision you already hold. Take two breaths, hold, and release. Now, allow Aventurine in. Moments into the system, Love creeps through, bending chakras so it is able to work into your framework. Then, you are able to embrace that Love is available to you. You can see Love in your eyes. "My life is full of Love," you repeat twice. Good. Take a break. Close the door. Return to this in a day. Just lie back, placing the crystal over your heart. Repeat the process as I described here. You feel warmth and devotion to Spirit. Perhaps, you feel waves of genuine

God-essence streaming through your eyes, the soul's windows. Appearing are stars. They welcome Love to your heart chakra. Call upon Archangel Shmuel. He is one to work in the ethers around heart Love. "Abysmal are the tidings when you have to try these experiments without an Archangel," Shmuel quips.

    I have more. It is here I ask for all the creatures of the Universe to assist Aventurine in providing numerous blessings to you when you choose her for healing assistance. The essence of Aventurine is a beauty and she enjoys attention. Along with Aventurine's energy, a myriad of angels works in the heavens to incorporate their blessed energy with your soul. There is a pure, blessed exchange that occurs when all are synched. If I provide remedies when angels are called, the work exponentially unfolds. So, call me and I will offer an enhanced experience so your work is manageable, balanced, blissful, and effectuated.

Azurite

- **"Third-Eye Chakra"**

Wow! This stone is a gem of a rock! What a crystal! Can you believe you own this? It's a wallapalooza! I enjoy working with her. She is a power ball socked in a garment looking like something you would find in a cave or mine.

"Hi!" says Azurite. "I'm going to explain who I am and you will see that I am unique in many ways. Work in a circular motion with me. I like to dance in a swirly fashion.

"The third eye is a powerful chakra because it manages the history of visions. Altercations are recorded. Demographics and other statistics are also put in volumes, or pages for historical reference. Today, I discuss how I can assist you in clearing third-eye visions that block your ability to see and know that danger is in sight. Place me between your eyes. It is easy to balance me on your forehead. With intention, please consider removing all hate towards those who were villainous. Danger inside can be removed with your desire to eliminate it from your soul. Okay. Take a breath. With the exhale, put out the

desire that visions of danger are eliminated. Forgive yourself, the ones who harmed you. Thank Spirit for lessons you were offered for soul growth. Now, take a breath. Rest. Good. Repeat when you wish to work on issues involving danger and villains—offenders of the spirit and issues that bring up fear to you when you rest your thoughts upon them. With each clearing session, work is done and more heaviness is eliminated from the third eye.

"'How do I know I'm done?' you ask me. I respond, "When you feel lightness of being. The fear you hold in the chakra affects your ability to work in safety. If you are burdened, you choose Azurite. I am your gal."

Bloodstone

- **"Root Chakra"**

First, I mention that the reference to the name is horrible. I eliminate the allusion to "dead," "all gone," "finito." This beaut is "out of here" in terms of it being one of a kind. It is unique. Bloodstone is terrific! I discuss its properties so you are able to use it efficiently.

A very soft, gentle tone is to be used when talking about Bloodstone. I whisper... Hush... Quiet... It is here; I can tune into the vibration. How do I feel when I touch her? She is rough, soft—in between both textures. What do you sense? It is your perception that matters here. Gentle when handling her. She needs reassurance that you know her and her abilities. Can you determine exactly how she senses that you are in synch with her? She vibrates "up" to get a hold of you, comes close, reads your "wave," and senses who you are. Anger will be sensed. So will hate, contempt, and boredom. Mistake not, she's a mind reader. Therefore, use your judgment when deciding whether your mind frame is solid and stable before working her into your healing day.

The root chakra is filled with debilitating energies when a person has not addressed issues related to family, law, justice, communication with the elements, etc. Many find themselves weak in the knees, cramping in the shins, and suffocating when outdoors due to allergies. These signs point to issues at the root level.

    Bloodstone is placed in the dominant hand. It can be held for long periods while you meditate and release cares associated with relationships, loyalty, and all related to survival. When you sit and clear problems associated with Love, you are basking in Love while healing. When you meditate and release issues about loyalty, survival, and all related to justice, multidimensional layers of Love come through to assist in the clearing. There are more layers that come through with root clearing. It is so. I share this so you have a good understanding of how Bloodstone works. "Layers" means times it takes to come through, repeat, and perform tasks to clear your energy wheel, or chakra. It is fabulous. Bloodstone comes in and bathes you. You are cherished throughout the process. Sit for an hour to release deep-seated issues. Hold up the hand to the window if you wish to charge it, too. Solar energy creates magnificent waves for a more attuned crystal. If you wish a short session, meditate for a few minutes, holding the vision that your situation will rectify shortly.

    Bloodstone is surely a wonderful crystal. I enjoy her. She is helpful to all who appreciate her wisdom. Remember: Hold her gently, whisper, and caress…

Blue Lace Agate

- **"Throat Chakra"**

This is the incredible crystal that bargains. It says, "How can I assist? Are you interested? Are you sure you're interested? If so, I have a proposition for you." Blue Lace Agate has a sense of humor. It sits, all pretty. It is a fashion plate, for sure. Yet, beneath the surface, there is a heart of gold. She is not the common, run-of-the-mill fashionista.

How do I say this? Okay. I will be blunt. She charms you into healing. Okay. It is said. I will go into detail. "Blue" is friendly and alluring. She takes a person and really has them enthralled by her appearance. Hmm. I am sure some sleep with her at night.

If I weave the throat chakra into this piece, I will say that when the energy of the crystal is activated, talking and feeling confident is enhanced. I feel her color has character. This enhances one's confidence, boosting their ability to open and speak.

Hold Blue in your hand (whichever one you prefer). Take a breath, hold, and release problems, whether they are financial, relational, physical, spiritual, or sexual. Home may be where you feel most comfortable doing this exercise. It is your choice; however, I believe your comfort is of utmost importance when working with Blue.

Now, imagine the space in your larynx (voice box) having an appearance of Light—a little opening where vibrations occur for speech. Fill the void with Light. Blue will shine itself in. Yes. You utter, "Come right on in, little one. Help me speak to my (fill in the blank with a person[s] of interest). Thank you." A minute of silence is essential. Please allow this time for Blue to shine in and assist in the release of issues preventing your successful communication with others.

Are there questions? Okay. You. There. "I wish to speak well. I crumble. How do I use Blue in this case?" Speak clearly. Delineate the issue. Allow the space to be filled with Light and Blue's beautiful energy. Imagine strength and fortitude working through the throat chakra. When you sit quietly, sensations are apparent. You need only sit for a minute, but this precious moment is valuable.

When you are done, take a minute to rest and reflect on what you chose to address for amelioration. She wishes reflection. It assists in the healing. This is key.

Carnelian

- **"Root Chakra"**

Carnelian. She is a beaut. What a stone. Can I describe the essence of a creature that bids *adieu* once it arrives? She is out of here. Truly. From the minute you are with her, she moves you tenderly away from your troubles. It is the, "I am gone"—her good-bye—that assists you in healing worries related to family. A friendship that is challenging, a person who commits you without supporting evidence—there are many specific situations she addresses. "Family" is the operative word and all persons you consider close, in your inner circle, will be addressed if you wish.

    Put her squarely in your palm. Hold the vision that "this relationship is healed." Release fear associated with boundaries, loyalties and comments said out of anger. Adjust your breathing. Slow it down. Concentrate on who it is you wish to focus on. The healing happens instantly. Many remark that Carnelian is magical in that it helps mend sorrow between souls. If your intent is genuine, you will find your relationships with friends or family members improve significantly. Thank her for her assistance. She appreciates this acknowledgement.

Celestite

- ## "Heart Chakra"

If you believe heartache is manifest when people are unable to find peace, listen to this advice about how Celestite can heal the sadness in your heart. He is a gem of a stone. Place him clear and center on your chest. Relax. Can you envision all sadness going away? If possible, imagine crystal energy streaming through to the consciousness that is your heart chakra. Celestite moves the issues that are unresolved and turns them into situations that can be looked at and released. When you are ready to absorb good, healing energy from "His Royal Highness," he'll lay you a golden egg that brings much relief to your system. Love is challenged on many levels and much work is done to resolve important issues that were not addressed and rectified until now. Your intention to heal is paramount to the efficacy of the work you do. Celestite needs grand entrances. Imagine worlds opening so it can enter in grand fashion. "Royal Highness Celestite is here! Come! Find me and assist me! I am here! Love is what I wish to address today!"

How often do you work in this manner? Use your discretion. It wishes respites because it becomes depleted with overuse. Energize Celestite by placing him in the light when the sun is high. He can rest for ten days in between workouts.

The next time you work with Celestite, offer gratitude and pray that all works out for the Highest Good of all.

• "Third-Eye Chakra"

If you find you are having difficulty perceiving how situations have come to be in such chaos, use Celestite for remediation. This stone offers great comfort with respect to healing wounds of vast proportions. Place Celestite in the center of your forehead, making sure it rests easily when lying prone. It is here you say a few intentional phrases asking for clarification about why, what, and how situations unraveled so. Can you mark a place on the timeline, recording when you believe a situation declined? I believe most can. This is how Celestite can assist you in determining how to heal situations that are fairly unmanageable to date.

What if the situation has transpired, yet you wish closure? The same applies here. Ask for clarification. Heal with forgiveness after identifying why, how, and when the situation fell apart and ended. If messages are not coming through, trust Celestite to work on releasing images to your consciousness. In time, the information is transferred so you are able to penetrate the Wall of Unknowing to feel comfort and peace.

Try this exercise: Place a hand over your crown chakra. Celestite can be on your third eye. Breathe in Divine Spirit, allowing Celestite to absorb much of the Holy Spirit. The magnificent radiance calls forth answers. Remove the images that prevent you from moving forward. This is good. Do this weekly in order to clear your third eye of debris that prevents you from shifting to more positive situations, venues, and relationships.

Citrine

- ## "Root Chakra"

What a picture! Do you see halos? I do. Citrine is a gem of a healer. Cohabitate with Citrine. It is a girl/guy's best friend. Okay. Enough accolades. It needs a more formal introduction. Citrine is a base-ic stone: It just sits at the base of the spine, pulling debris out. Simple. Put the crystal on a ledge and watch it shine. Using intention, take this energy and shift it to your base, or root chakra. Imagine many glints of solid rays shining on the stone. You can intentionally pick up the rays that sat on Citrine and place them below your navel. If you allow Citrine to pull out negative energy, you will feel renewed. Worries related to Love, health, happiness are somewhat quelled. If you can place this crystal on the root chakra, you will find yourself sitting calmly and peacefully after a short time. This is all you need to do. Citrine is a "Master Healer"; it is able to clear debris easily, effortlessly, and without haste. Can you try to place a bit of Citrine there and meditate for ten minutes, casting the intention your daily worries are quelled?

- ## "Sacral Chakra"

The color of the stone varies, yet Citrine tends to be yellow to orange in hue. It is powerful for many reasons. One is to clear the sacral chakra of negative energy. My job is to offer you objects to utilize in the healing of self. Citrine, which is used to clear the sacral, is so powerful that many find it quite overwhelming. Can you envision using it at your discretion? Please be advised that Citrine is used sparingly.

When you place the crystal over your abdomen, do so with respect. It likes peace. This object of great strength only wants to be treated with the utmost respect.

Tune into your breathing. It is here you carefully attune yourself to Citrine and the power it holds. All issues related to creative force and control are addressed and released if your spirit wishes this removal. The idea of using Citrine for chakra clearing is simple: Take issues of irresolution—both conscious and unconscious—and intend they are released. This will free up any obstacles that impede your projects from being completed.

It is always a good idea to cast doubts aside when trying new methods to increase your energy. After releasing any doubts about the process, fill the void with optimism and excitement. Then, your work will be enhanced.

• "Solar Plexus Chakra"

"The first time I ever..." This is what many speak when they refer to the time they first began using Citrine for power and prosperity. People remark the stone is a keeper. I recommend using this crystal for all issues that relate to abundance and strength of character.

Citrine is unique. It amplifies while it also deflects energy. The good energy is enhanced and the negative energy is wasted, or washed away. It is so. I suggest you place Citrine clearly over your stomach, above your belly and below the rib cage. This soft spot in the crook of your gut by your diaphragm is the area I speak of. Now, distress is to be dissolved. Imagine full removal of all stress related to control and sadness. It takes a while to dissolve, so be patient. When the image of sadness is gone, you will feel lighter. This is so. It is a good idea to try experiments with Citrine around power issues. Take different methods of healing, for example. You test them to see what works better for you. The same applies with Citrine and how it is applied to solar plexus healing. If Citrine is held in the hand, does this work more effectively than if it is placed on the chakra itself? If Citrine is held in the air and sunlight is captured in its essence, does this serve you better? Try new ways of using this crystal. I believe the experimentation allows you to feel empowered, which is *exactly what I wish to achieve for your healing.*

Clear Calcite

"All Chakras"

Healers often use Calcite, yet they do not fully understand how it clears debris. What is important to understand is that Calcite is quick and dirty. It pulls debris up very quickly. When you apply the crystal to your chakras, there is immediate release.

The first time you do this, rest before applying the crystal to your body. The image you wish to hold is that of peace. Can you sit, resting quietly? If not, do not proceed. It is necessary to be quiet and still before your healing session. If you have readied yourself with quietude, then continue. Each chakra is like a bird: One feather sits on top of another, stacked, flitting in place. A bird also waits for the removal of issues that are deep and longstanding. If its feathers are ruffled, the process is flimsy, at best. Set the intention that you can do this easily.

Choose a chakra you feel requires attention. It is the responsibility of the cardholder to remove issues expediently. "God. Maker. Please remove the source of pain that prevents me from proceeding. I wish full release. Thank you." Your job is to repeat this till you feel a shift. Seconds have lapsed. You have said this a few times. Now, you move on. If nothing is perceived, it is okay. It is not necessary to feel, know, or see change.

The next chakra is easy because you have released issues from the first chakra. Continue in this manner until all seven chakras have been spoken of. If there is a question about how long to spend on each chakra, feel secure in knowing that ten seconds per chakra is all that is necessary.

Calcite is powerful. It remedies all sorts of ills, from pain to insecurity. You need to know that the issues are expelled as fast as they were asked to leave. Shifts are huge. Drink water after this healing, for the body rids itself of waste (debris) from the lifetimes that were addressed.

I recommend using Calcite if you wish emergent issues to be resolved. I also feel Calcite rids pain quickly. When there is an issue of immediacy, use him. He does not disappoint.

Clear Quartz

"All Chakras"

She sits atop a mountain. She is strong. Unbreakable. Each chakra is healed when she descends from the mountain peak and enters your being. Clear Quartz is phenomenal. She is a beast, a gift of strength. When she aligns your root, sacral—the core—up through the Divine opening at the head, you feel light and happy.

All you do is sit quietly. Imagine a solar light—a panel facing you. Sit Clear Quartz across from you in a way where you face her directly. Each chakra is visible to her. Breathe in and allow Clear Quartz to beam Love on you like the solar light you imagine. It takes time, a few seconds for it to come in your system. Give an exhale and relax. It has taken hold. Good. It is working through the chakras. When you inhale, the activation is set. Exhaling allows the energy to penetrate and work through layers of lifetimes of pain.

When is a good time to stop? Well, it takes time for Clear Quartz to make its way up the pathway to the crown chakra. Ten minutes is a good amount of time. Yes. Work with her. She allows you to take moments to rest, too. In

between cycles, she will push you away where you will wish a respite. Close your eyes. Rest. Take a break. Then return to her for more work. In a matter of speaking, she is an accommodating friend. Very flexible and willing to be there when you wish her assistance.

Light enters her. She casts a glow. Each "muscle" in her body is drenched with Love. Her essence is Light. She becomes tired from this work. Allow her to cleanse herself by putting her near the window. Place her carefully in the box when you are done. Rays of Light offer her strength and renewal. By the next day, she is recharged and willing to descend from the mountain again. "Peace to you. Peace," she says. She means it, and she delivers, too.

Diamond

- ## "Heart Chakra"

I LOVE Diamond! I love the way Diamond shines bright and clear so you see reflections of Love all around you. He can be a she, depending on how you look at him/her. Take a moment to consider that the Love you feel is a combination of Love that is both masculine and feminine in nature. Diamond is so balanced with both male and female energy that one need not believe he finds true Love for a man or she only seeks out Mr. Right for her. We have a beautiful duo here for you.

The Love Diamond brings in is powerful. I say this with reverence. Please know it is the prudent crystal card carrier who uses this energy wisely. "All things come to those who wait," said a philosopher of old. Today, I say this holds true if you consider using Diamond as a life changer. If you believe he/she can shift your soul, it will be so. I say this with utmost respect. Diligence is necessary if you desire massive change.

Take Diamond and place him/her over your heart. Your heart beats regularly. With Diamond atop your chest, it may speed some. If you are uncomfortable, remove him/her from your body. Take time to balance yourself so you may return to the clearing of your heart chakra. If you speed again, drink water. Return only when there is no sensation of a sped-up heartbeat. When you are in a comfortable position, please allow Diamond to work on you. It takes fifteen to twenty seconds for the energy to enter you. After that, imagine much work is done. *Rev. Rev. Hum…* There is a speedy quality to the work. In, out. Pull out debris. Release. In for more. Pull out, release. In, out. You see? Like gears or pistons working quickly. While in a comfortable, relaxed state, take time to ask Diamond to assist in the release of sadness in your heart. Reflect, like the way Light reflects on a surface when sun hits it. Reflect. Imagine you float and all troubles are securely removed from your chakra. If you wish Love to enter in your life, place the intention she or he enters your life in a manner that is smooth and fluid. If you worry, release. If you doubt, release. All obstacles in manifesting your Love are to be dealt with. Examine life today. Eliminate your concerns and allow all to enter in a wondrous manner.

I believe you are ready for Love. What say you? Have you reflected on what you wish and how you can eliminate what stands in your way? Okay. Now, rest. Just sit back and allow Diamond to work through you. In a few days after your chakra clearing work, you may feel light and bright. Your reflection of yourself may be different, meaning how you see yourself as a Divine soul may shift. Your attitude about Love, lovers may also change. Enjoy the attunement!

• "Third-Eye Chakra"

The person who changes is you. You find time to shift. Using objects like crystals is one way to heal. We find this method of self-healing beautiful. How clever to release past woes with assistance from Diamond.

The tissue in the eye is made of a vitreous solution. It is very valuable. This liquid assists in establishing sight. Now, the eye known as the "third eye" is a structure that enables one to see—truly see what lies before them. Diamond is the tool that eliminates debris obstructing your view of the virtual reality in which you live and breathe.

Take a few seconds to place Diamond on the spot above your eyes in the middle of your forehead. Let it rest there for a few seconds. If you wish minutes, please do. Then, wipe away the debris. Allow, with intention, your mind to sweep the debris—anger, sadness, waste of any kind—from this chakra. Crying may ensue and this is to be expected. Much is lifted when Diamond is in your third eye. Blink and begin the process five minutes later. Place Diamond on your forehead and intentionally remove anger and sadness from the third-eye chakra. If you do this several times in fifteen minutes, resting for five minutes between clearings, you have done well. Rest, drink water, and return to your activities. The third eye wishes to resume activity from before your healing work began.

This is a generous method of healing; the body allows much to be released by intention. There is a lot you have stored inside. With your assistance, Diamond flushes and pulls out debris from this chakra. Powerful healing energy is replaced where damage might have occurred. Know that the method used is comparable to taking water and dumping it out when it is stagnant. It is replaced with fresh liquid. Particles of Light shine on it to absorb any residue that might be left after the flushing.

Diamond congratulates you for your excellent accomplishment. Continue this process on a weekly basis if you desire much clarity in your life. Your view of life shifts when the third eye is unencumbered. Enjoy the view!

Emerald

- **"Heart Chakra"**

Emerald calms the soul of the person who is living wildly. She is a change agent. Use Emerald if you are feeling out of sorts, sad, confused, or bonkers. I repeat: If you are "out there"—just wild and needing a respite—use Emerald. She is a facilitator of calmness. I recommend that heart-based issues be addressed here. Emerald prefers to be used when Love is in question. All your concerns—wanting to be married, living with the boy- or girlfriend, finding stillness when your heart breaks, or loving one's self—are on the table.

To begin this work, I ask that all pendants be removed. If you wear jewels, take them and put them in a drawer. All the energy you are currently feeling is to be kept within; your jewels absorb frequencies that are better left inside versus absorbed. It can take days till your body settles, so plan to be jewelry-free till then.

I recommend sitting in a very sunny place near a window when using Her Grace. If you are sad, she removes it during meditation. Relax and breathe. Much of what you address is based on old beliefs and issues that have not been resolved. Karma is worked on. Issues surface for you to look at and release. Go inside and list your concerns. Write on your mind's eye all that you wish to address and Emerald will reveal to you what is necessary to be released. If

you choke, snort, ache, or cry in pain, it is Emerald who is taking pain from your heart chakra.

When Emerald is working, she emits a frequency of high caliber. Very intense. So much so that angels talk in a whisper when she is activated. We hear her sing in Heaven.

The heart skips. It paces itself and is now aligned. The work is done. Use Emerald if you need quick fixes. It jump-starts situations and turns them around, as well, with the blink of an eye.

Carry Emerald close to you when you use her. She needs your faith that you are both intertwined as "Love-makers" during your session. When your work is done, thank Her Excellence and graciously place her back in the box. She returns the gesture with a dear kiss, nod, and wink.

Fluorite

"All Chakras"

Fluorite manages systemic problems that are having a strong effect on you. This crystal is rock solid when it comes to healing woes. Fluorite is genuine; she loves her work as a healer. Truly. She sits atop the Pyramid of Light, producing special rays that work through chakras, eliminating suffering in fell swoops. This crystal is beautiful and is useful at times of crisis, as well as when you feel very low and hopeless. Why stop here? She mimics tribes in the Orient with her perfume—all spiced and ready for travel. Her journey is to your doorstep. She wishes to provide comfort in a fancy and exotic way that is unique and quite satisfying.

Place Fluorite over heat before you use her. It can be sunshine, a heated plate, or your hand. This enlivens her being. After seconds of engagement, put Her Majesty over your head. First, take some breaths. Imagine she enters your crown chakra, moving slowly down the space inside your body. Relieve pressure by then placing her against a mirror so she is facing you. She works well from this position. (The rest of the healing takes place with her being near you, instead of above you.)

Several minutes go by. You sit, meditating on your troubles. Ask Archangel Michael for assistance. He will provide sanctuary that is needed while you release all that supports terror and pain. He assists while Fluorite combs the chakras of pain. They work in tandem. This is so. When you feel light, please thank her for her assistance. Archangel Michael appreciates the recognition, yet he believes credit is placed with dear Fluorite.

Come to the head of the class. Use Fluorite to step up and feel better. It is possible to achieve a new sense of "the good life" with her in your healing toolbox.

Galena

- ## "Root Chakra"

The first time you find a piece of Galena, you smile. "What a lovely piece of life." I smile. I find this object so wonderful. I enjoy the texture. Run your hands over this gorgeous piece of life. It is *magnifique*.

I have much to say about her: She is genuine in her Love of all beings. She sits, smiles, waits for people to hold her in their arms, caressing her sides. "How sensual," you remark. I abruptly respond, "Yes. She is a Love, a true Love."

Let's take time to learn about Her Grace. She has energy cascading down her sides like waterfalls. Each ridge cascades and multiplies energy to the next silvery level. If you wait a while between holding her in your arms, you will feel sad that she is away from you. Try to control yourself. She is intoxicating.

The energy released in layers goes to your root, as it is to strengthen the base chakra. If you hold a level (the measuring tool) and watch the bubble go to center, she watches in excitement. The bubble is Galena. She needs you to be in balance. If you are off kilter, she sways. She moves and sways to encourage energy to return to center. If Galena is upset, it is because you are releasing old wounds related to warrior-like loyalty. It is the dismantling of constructs that allows balance to come to the fore.

Have you released all you can today? If so, Galena will wait for you until you wish a cleanse of the root again. If you wish her assistance, she prefers your attention on her alone. Remove all distractions. A room with light is important. Electricity bothers her, so please unplug units that radiate waves blocking her

work. She is ready. Your hand holds the card with her name. Palm faces her picture. You rest comfortably. Allow her to instruct you how to proceed. So, imagine you instruct Galena how to sift through layers of pain and sorrow within your chakra. As you intuit and guide her, you wash yourself of old muck and debris. Take control. You are the most important person. You have found a way to relieve yourself of tension. Transmit hope to your root chakra, reassuring it that many times you let it be, but now you address its needs. This honoring of the past and the neglect of your needs is important work. Please praise yourself for giving the gift of time to heal yourself. Galena praises you. She comments on your bravery and fortitude.

For now, you heal your root chakra with Galena. Another day, you choose another crystal. Each level you reach in healing marks another moment when you have left behind what confounded life and shifted your base chakra so your needs are met more comfortably, safely, and joyfully.

After you work with Galena, drink water, rest, and ask angels and Spirit to guide you to your next healing adventure.

Garnet

- ## "Root Chakra"

Garnet is ready, willing, and able to be there for you as you work on issues that complicate basic functioning. She helps you face strife, conflict, boredom, safety, self-preservation, home life, and attitudes about family and children. If you engage her services, she will lift and support this chakra that also focuses on nutrition, sleep, and rest. Diet is addressed, first and foremost, so remember to eat before working with her.

Place Garnet in a window where sunlight radiates on her. The energy strengthens and supports her ability to address you. Then, set her near you, up to one foot away, where you believe her being picks up your energy. With a few breaths, relax. Diet and exercise are addressed: Her soft energy enters the base of your spine into the middle of the chakra. Imagine leaving wounds behind. Sorrow is lifted. Cleanse your aura (energy field outside your body) by imagining salt sprinkled on top of your head. Sit and weep if you wish. It is safe. Healing occurs on many levels. Sleep issues are addressed: Garnet puts a coating of Love inside the root chakra. She is able to strengthen the unit's functioning with this "gear." Each person is then "outfitted" with an armor of sorts that increases their ability to face fear and sorrow. Much angst is transmuted as the armor settles into its rightful place. The wheel of the chakra slows to allow this settling. Take a drink of pure water at this time. The *aqua* strengthens the work.

Please step back from the position you sit in, close your eyes and "sleep" in space. Float. If you are unable, Garnet will assist and you, unknowingly, will lift up so the gem can enter underneath your chakra. The work here is delicate. Ten minutes is how long this procedure takes. After this period, you may rest. She put messages in your spine, at the base of your soul, to remind you Love is within – eternally incorporated and part of your fabric. Before your healing session with Garnet closes, she stretches and cries for release of all hurt – all pain and sorrow accumulated over lifetimes. If you thank her, she beams and also sheds tears of joy that you accepted her gifts. She is easily moved. Drink water and remember to rest. You have done much work.

- "Heart Chakra"

Garnet catches your eye in the dark like a lantern that hangs ready for you to reach out and take hold of its energy. She is mighty and illuminates darkness. In her possession is a beautiful babe, of sorts – a cocooned, wrapped infant she holds close to her. As she rests, she nurses this babe. When you hold the crystal, it carries the message of birth, rebirth, Love, and genuine soulful compassion.

Work with Garnet to free angst. If your heart cries for help, she is here. In an instant, she emits rays of hope. Hold her very close to your bosom and just sit. Allow her to enter. Close your eyes and dream how you wish your situation to resolve. Envision a chapter ending beautifully. Imagine new beginnings – that all is well. She emits sounds and echoes that transmute pain. Lively little ripples fly through the ethers and charge your heart chakra, filling it with Light. It is important you rest and feel calm during Garnet's work with you.

After you have fallen into a deep slumber, a lull, please take Garnet and put her in a place where she is away from others. She prefers solitude. When you feel she has had time to cleanse herself, place her with the other crystals. She finds respites important after working in your heart. Thank her. She enjoys acknowledgment and appreciates your words of gratitude. When you return to your activities, eat a light meal. If you find yourself happy, light, and free, it is Garnet who assisted in moving you to this place of sanctuary and peace.

Gold

- ## "Solar Plexus Chakra"

What is more than the best of the utmost of all things found in the universe? I say Gold is the treasure you have searched for and found. Place a piece of him inside your palm. The card reads "Gold," so this is what your palm is to see. Place another hand atop the card so it is embraced by both palms, cradled in Love. Darkness is what Gold prefers. It enjoys healing the soul in quiet, closed spaces. Your cupped hands provide the environment it desires.

Whisper words of hush, peace to this instrument of beauty called Gold. Each spoken word gives it a tingle of excitement and pleasure. Joy emanates from its being. Are you focused on the issues pertaining to how you feel weak? Place your attention on power struggles, weakness of spirit, and times when you fell in the face of fear. Bottled emotions are gathered and swept aside as Gold works through you. He takes time, sifting and gathering unwanted "emblems" that mark you as undesirable, childish, and unworthy. These names are tattered and removal is easy. Please assist Gold by wishing that all times of hopelessness and despair be removed and sent to the Light.

I join Gold during this process. We work together, hand in hand. I, the alchemist, move energy to make this process occur. Like a catalyst, I work silently and smoothly.

    Turn the card over and read the words I have spoken. Repeat this a few times until you know it by heart. Close your eyes and see whether there are lingering thoughts of sadness, weakness, or hopelessness. Attune yourself to Gold again by placing him face down on your palm. Repeat this until you have a light feeling about you.

    Digestive issues often arise when working with Gold. He makes you burp and pass gas as a way to release what has been pent up for many years, or possibly lifetimes. Antacids and other remedies quell discomfort, yet the object is to release instead of stifle what is occurring. Lay low, emit sounds of displeasure, and allow all to flow through as it should. Work of this nature can make you tired, so sleep if you need to. All is perfect when you wake in the morning, rested and ready for life to unfold as it does.

    Thank Gold. He enjoys warm and heartfelt words of gratitude. Bless yourself for the work you did. It is I who blesses you, too, for Gold and I believe your efforts to heal yourself are worth praise and recognition.

Granite

- **"Root Chakra"**

"All come to order. Please stand, for Granite is entering chambers." The Winston Churchill of rocks, this remedy works. I do not mince words here. Granite is all you bargained for. What a stone. I see her as magnificent: shiny, sturdy, solid, and strong.

Here is a list of her qualifications:

- She dives into your root chakra in a single bound.
- She leaves no issue unturned.
- She whispers words of hope so you may feel relief.
- She enters and exits quickly, performing miracles that account for many life changes afterwards.

After you have read this list and sat with Granite, take her and hold her near you. Your heart is a good place to begin. Earth's energy surges up to join Granite at your heart. Much upliftment occurs now. Take her and sit with her by your side. Just rest. Imagine she is like an author—writing, scribing on you a lot of information that works as a treatment on your psyche. This information goes very deep into old wounds. The root chakra sits, absorbing every word that is transcribed onto it. The root chakra rests because so much is being said. It hears and knows what is happening.

As soon as it is time, the chakra bursts open and releases old habits—ones that are basic to survival. These are habits that were unhealthy, keeping you from health and wealth. All the energy that is released comes out in waves. Drink water at this time, sipping slowly. Now rest.

It is a journey one goes on when using Granite for healing. The path is not too long; it is one half hour of cleansing with her. Find ways to sit in different positions so you maximize her strength. If you are cross-legged, get up, move, and return to legs unfolded. Sit in an armchair, then on the sofa. The movement is important because she requires numerous turns inward and needs a new vantage point from which to enter. It is personal on her part—simply a preference or style of healing you.

The goal of the work is to release all wounds involved in self-minimization related to basic survival. You know much work has been accomplished when you see changes that involve household issues, family, and old relationships. Many issues may come apart and untangle, working out for the better if you view this in this way. Foraging for Love may disappear. New situations present themselves. It is a new beginning for you.

Hematite

- *"Root Chakra"*

Dropping Hematite is like expecting the Hindenburg to float in water. It sinks. Do not drop Hematite. "Clunk" is the last sound it wishes to make. So, I say this as you prepare your work with dear ol' pal, Hematite.

He is a crystal of true power. He works hard to calm wounds that date to times gone by. If you believe he can trap negative energy, remove old issues related to people who abused you and told you that you were nothing but a mess, then your work will be quite successful.

I believe you will find Hematite to be a dense material. The card you hold has "weight." The density is something to be reckoned with and honored. Place Hematite directly near a window to absorb the sun's energy. Very smart to bathe it in Light before healing yourself.

Now, sit and rest near the window. The light shining through captures what you are releasing. Hematite is sitting, propped in your lap like a coddled baby. Stretch your legs. Energy is released. Sit and rest. Remind Hematite you are releasing wounds of days gone by. It is your job to allow the essence of this stone

to delve deep into your soul. The root chakra is addressed in quite a Heavenly fashion: Hematite dives and excavates beautifully like Esther Williams, the famous swimmer movie star. Before you can say, "I'm ready for a nap," this stone has assisted in releasing wounds you chose to discard.

You will know after a while when to stop the clearing work. Close your eyes, locate a focal point in your mind and place your cares to rest. "All is well. I am calm." This completes your session. You can relax, drink water and reflect on what might have been released. At this time, a smile emanates from your soul. Trust that you are moving forward and are ready for more challenges when your spirit sends you back to the card deck.

Jade

- **"Heart Chakra"**

It is a perfect match, Jade and you. Take the matrimonial blessing, "With this ring, I thee wed," visualize removing the "ring" and place Jade on your finger. She is a stone that harmonizes your heart. Sing and she echoes the notes. They are strong.

Your heart needs Jade to remove any sadness that sits inside. It is a convoluted process if you look at it closely. There are frequencies that sit in the heart chakra that need to be attuned to Jade before working together. So, place a magnet near the crystal card. Let it sit for ten to fifteen minutes. The frequencies sitting in the heart will need amplification. Jade receives emissions from the magnet. Trust this occurs on a very deep soul level. Jade welcomes the magnet's assistance. Now, very carefully, place Jade on your heart chakra (the center of your chest). Slowly, turn on a switch inside you where you imagine wounds relating to rape, incest, depraved indifference to life, slavery, and all situations where one might encounter debauchery and death. Jade removes feelings of betrayal, sadness, fear, and sleep issues (deprivation, insomnia, interrupted sleep). If you close your eyes, it works more efficiently.

Oftentimes, people experience great pleasure—a sense of relief—after Jade has called out the wounds and released them to Spirit. Joy has been felt by

some after she has attended to them. Whatever feeling(s) you experience, it is perfect. You have done well. Your Higher Self permits Jade to go in and find what is bothering you and has bothered you from other lifetimes.

You can ask her to speak if you wish. Some can hear her words if they listen closely. Her messages are audible and crisp. We attune you so you can hear her speak. The deaf are able to hear her because words are translated into symbols. Sounds do not have to be spoken in order to communicate with Jade.

Allow time in between healings, as Jade needs rest before returning to work. The moment you call her name she is ready to assist. So, call upon her and know she is a giver, oftentimes forgetting she does need a nap. In light of this, she will accommodate your schedule, as long as you respect her requiring time for rejuvenation. Thank you for respecting her wishes. Enjoy Jade. She is a keeper.

Kyanite

"All Chakras"

Take time to sit. Just rest. Close your eyes. Kyanite energy is very soothing. You need a dose of Kyanite to relieve stress. This "stress relief capsule" is prescribed for all who want to rest and relax. Each time you use her, all chakras stand up and release what ails them. Kyanite energy is pure and smooth. Wish that each time you hold her she gently releases your concerns. Now, let me begin the discussion about how the work is done.

Kyanite has a presence that commands one to listen to her. Hold your palm face up. Place her in your hand and slowly close your fingers around her. Caress her. She desires Love and this is what motivates her. With your heart attuned to the center of her being, allow her to move through you. Your center—your core—is exactly what gets addressed. Each chakra stands at attention while she waves, or glides to them. If you see a creature in the deep blue sea stand upright while their slippery tentacles wave back and forth to the water's rhythm, you will appreciate Kyanite's force, her way of passing through the chakras. The journey is slow; each chakra is given full attention. Five or so minutes will do for each chakra, so plan a good half hour or more for this healing exercise.

When you are finished, release Kyanite from your hand. Place her in a dish. The oils from your hand accumulate on her and she needs to be wiped off. When you have cleaned her, bless and thank her for her healing assistance. When you go to sleep at night, your dream state will be very lively. You will feel busy, yet the moment you wake you will realize the previous day's work with Kyanite enabled you to have rest—a very good night's sleep.

Great is her work! I appreciate how she graciously accepts all opportunities to assist those who need rest and deep cleansing of their soul. I thank you for the work you do and find you courageous in allowing Kyanite to go inside and help make your experience more perfect than it already is.

Labradorite

"All Chakras"

I will say that Labradorite is very similar to that of a meteor. It showers over the chakra pathway, dissolving, blessing, and then finally creating a stream, or "flow through" chasm that is optimal for restoring one's energy. As she moves through the pathway, there is an arc of Light that is quite substantial. Remarkable. Sit and listen to the vibe she emits; it resonates with birds in flight. Whenever there is a humming sensation, know she is working to restore balance along the pathway.

How you choose to sit with her is your decision. You make the rules. Labradorite waits to be beckoned as a child sits waiting for the teacher to call them to the front of the class. If you choose a hand to hold her in, the right one is optimal. If you sit beside her, give her some space; on top of you is not her preference. Now, breathe some cool, deep breaths and open your eyes. Keep them open, for it is now that she streams into your head, the crown chakra. Beneath the surface lie "gems" to be polished. Each chakra is a gem; she refines them with a twist and turn motion unlike other stones. The Labradorite I know has many faces, yet she is typically known to work in a gyrating manner.

Sit and allow Labradorite to examine each chakra carefully. Just allow time to pass. You will feel peace and joy after a while if you sit with her regularly. By the time she has finished with your root chakra, a sense of urgency or rushing to complete the task of healing may come upon you. Do not worry. You are finished for today. Examine how you feel now as compared to when you first began your session. I do hope a sensation of relief is upon you at this moment. Indeed, a thorough cleansing of your energy system has occurred. Drink water. Allow for the healing to settle in. Be mindful of your breath; deep breathe if you are shallow in breath. The oxygen helps restore any residual imbalances that are present. Proceed through your day and enjoy the beauty that has awakened inside you. Labradorite enjoys her sessions. She wholeheartedly hopes you succeed in your endeavors and find joy in all you do.

Lapis Lazuli

- ## "Throat Chakra"

If you were to place this beauty on your neck, information would stream inside where throat chakra issues are stored. In many lifetimes, you have grappled with throat concerns, whether they be tearing up and stifling a sob, choking on your words, or using epithets to spew on a friend who crossed you. Find solace in knowing that Lapis Lazuli is here to console you. He breaks up rage in a fell swoop, knocking through dense layers that are difficult to break through in ordinary fashion.

Take Lapis Lazuli and hold him squarely in your palm. The sensation of Love comes through as you allow him to work into your soul. Each layer that is peeled reflects a lifetime of events that inhibited you from feeling and being a communicative member in the universe. Hold him a few times, trading hands for an even distribution of "events release." As you swap hands, imagine he is working on balancing you. Throat pain you might experience is normal. If the release is sudden and a whoosh of discomfort ekes through to your consciousness, drink water. The crystal is powerful and not for the light of heart. Begin your session with Lapis Lazuli again after a few days of meditation. This is necessary. You provide your energy system a chance to remember what has transpired and what has been released. Drink water to flush the memories from the physical body. Sleep if you feel drowsy; the release comes in many forms.

The talented Lapis Lazuli wishes you a speedy recovery, so use him when you are strong. The weak are not to work with him due to his forceful style. Thank you for heeding my suggestion.

- ## "Third-Eye Chakra"

Lapis is patient and kind. He keys into you, shifts, and streams his energy based on exactly how you feel.

The third eye is sensitive. "Wash" this card before placing Lapis on your face. Use intention to clear the energy. Handle him carefully. You will release carbon atoms that interfere with the healing. Your third eye is ready to be worked on when you are. Get comfortable. Sit in a chair. Cross-legged is okay, as well, if you choose to sit somewhere else. Allow Lapis to remove images in your mind. The sadness, confusion, and tiredness you have is to be mitigated. Eliminate your eye's worries. Just allow this crystal to work diligently. He is patient. Just relax. A little (release) goes a long way.

You see improvement as the treatments unfold. Each sitting allows you to go inside and eliminate deep concerns involving seeing and knowing what is right and wrong. Injustice is addressed. Shame and guilt are, as well. Each pass over the third eye chakra gives you more clarity of vision. The clearing of this chakra affords you the opportunity to see how all is clear, despite the muck and mire you perceive around you. Enjoy working with this Master stone.

Malachite

Before you try a healing with her, Malachite needs to be washed. Take your energy—the intention that you are cleansing a crystal—and apply it to the card. If you doubt your ability, go in and remedy this. It is of great importance that she be clear of residue from readings done before this day. When you are clear and able to cleanse Malachite, please do so. She wants perfection in her healing, so you need to perform this rite well.

- ## "Solar Plexus Chakra"

Raise the roof! Malachite takes and shakes the core! Hurry! Mom calls! Get the stone! Malachite wants to see you stand up to her, so begin!

The lesson here is this: Create a place where Love enters and no one is hurt. I say this softly, for some cannot be strong without creating disturbance. The balanced way to achieve Mastery in strength is to work through issues of power. Malachite takes the helm. Follow her lead.

Place her in the middle of your body, below the rib cage. Enjoy peace and quiet. She enters a tunnel below the skin's surface, ravaging opponents, or obstacles that bleed you of strength. Call upon Archangel Raphael to remove layers of deceit, sadness, betrayal, and lust. This is done through intending she enters your aura (energy field outside the physical body) and goes directly to the solar plexus chakra.

Drink water. It assists in the process. Music is effective in allowing energy to flow directly to this place where hurt resides. Disturbing music is unadvisable. Peace is what you wish to achieve. When you have concluded that Malachite entered, devoured, and removed energy that kept you weak, you are done. The healing ends with praying. "Goddess, Master of Heavenly Help and Love, please take my offering of thanks. I assume responsibility for what I do today and wish to continue healing in your footsteps." With grace and dignity, you share these words with her.

On a profound level, Malachite found pieces of your soul so bitter that some angels prefer Malachite does this work. This is tremendous. She stands strong. She wishes you follow suit.

- **"Heart Chakra"**

If you are sad or longing for Love, please sit and write two things that upset you. Then, place the list on the card. Malachite assumes that you wish these issues to be resolved and returned to Source. When you are ready to release them, a feeling of warm, pure, solid energy overwhelms you. Take a moment to pray. Ask God, The One who delivers angels to assist you, to heal everything in relation to your concerns. Now, place Malachite over your heart chakra where dreams are kept. It is here she removes the layers of strong urges and deep beliefs that kept you from being content. Be peaceful at this time. Much work is accomplished.

When you are done, the fear and the longing have a different face. You could almost feel new. Place Malachite in a room that is clean and free of stirrings. Quietude is her request after her work is completed. Now, you need time to sit and rest, as well. You must occupy a separate room. Find solitude and go within. It is a chance to be free and calm. Malachite continues to work ethically on you for an hour afterwards, despite your physical separation. Drink water with lemon in it for clarifying your system. Enjoy this treat of a healing.

Obsidian

- ## "Root Chakra"

When monuments are built, Obsidian is often chosen to be mixed into concrete. Pieces of the stone are used to construct edifices, which she fortifies. Her strength, her will to succeed emanates from her being, her essence.

Many projects are accomplished when she is chosen to be an assistant. Take Obsidian, lay her down in the middle of a table. Bless the area you work on. If your shirt is dirty, a skirt worn, please remove them in exchange for attire that is crisp and new. Obsidian, the Queen, enjoys ritual. She would rather you take time to prepare for her arrival than throw her down, asking her for help.

When you have found time to sit still and meditate, she will release you from suffering. From when you began the process of placing her on the table, she began taking time to connect with you. How does she know what to do? A little practice—eons of time—made her quite adept at reading energy.

How does it feel to sit watching Obsidian take away basic troubles such as pain and suffering from childhood? How do you experience this? Some meander in their thoughts as she works through layers of guilt. Some cry. Still, others find a moment to eat a snack during the healing session.

When you are done, notice the energy in the room. Find peace knowing you cleared yourself, as well as the area you now reside in. Heaven collapses structures where pain unequivocally hurts family and friends equally with you. Rest. Take time to clear the table, using intention, of any feeling you have that might interfere with moving forward in a positive and healthy manner. You are done with the healing session at this time. Pray that the moment you walk out the door you will enter as a new soul yearning for ample opportunity to grow and receive more than when you left.

Opal

- ## "Crown Chakra"

Find the luminescence. Ahh... It is brilliant. Opal is a stone that can take you far off to a land of make-believe. This crystal is best used to fly past galaxies, meandering far, far away. Take your hat off and put Opal square on your head. If this is not possible, intend it sits there where your crown chakra resides. Put all the focus on your head, for the crown chakra that connects to All That Is will be addressed in this healing session.

Please consider taking all issues related to life and God and place them in the middle of your crown chakra. If you leave any issues out, this is to be expected. Make a point to connect with Mother Earth by grounding yourself. Imagine roots extending below your feet, capturing her energy. This enables the energy to flow up the chakras. The point of this is to capture God above as is below.

When you connect with God, It circles your aura, entering the surface first as It glides in for a landing. Take a breath. Work through distrust and disbelief of all related to God, Heaven, and angels. Death is exactly as it appears: an illusion. All is destroyed as issues are deconstructed. New images and concepts

are introduced to replace false beliefs. When you have time to reflect on your issues about Love as it relates to God and all creatures, you can be sure your chakra gets a dose of cleansing so pure that you will cry with Joy.

Many issues were eliminated after they were addressed and reviewed. Opal's work is quick. She is swift with interpreting information you store in the crown. By the time the healing is complete—approximately ten minutes or so—many past issues are gone and have returned to Source.

Drink water after this session. Opal needs a refresher, too, so place her in sunshine when you can. The Light cleanses her soul. Thank you for working swiftly to release the blocks between you and The Oneness.

Orange Calcite

- **"Sacral Chakra"**

This is a very perfect stone. The color excites all who set their eyes on it. First, take a moment to feel the quality of the surface. Gaze at her. She wishes that you creep your eyes along her back, watching how she sits so statuesquely. The ripples, or cones moving through her body generate energy like a lynx moving so captivatingly in the evening sunset.

For the purposes of healing, please hold Orange Calcite close to you. She needs to be held. All her days are spent caring for those who sadly sit, mournfully so. The energy comes through Egyptian princes as she works to release pain in the sacral chakra. Hold her. Imagine she wriggles to the core of your gut, below the belly button. Residing here are concepts, or issues of abandonment, jealousy, and longing. Contempt is removed. Many people find this method of healing satisfying and energetically pleasurable. The color exuding from her is warm, pure, and freeing.

The time to work with Orange Calcite is when you feel empty and insecure—plenty tired and overwhelmed by situations involving work. The family issues at home contribute to the overwhelming feelings you experience. Here is how you can utilize her best: Take her and cradle the Love that is she. Hold Orange Calcite. The tears flow. Pain is released. Just hold her. She patiently waits till you are done releasing all that bothers you. Do not rely on a timer to indicate when to stop. She slows down until no more is left to release. You then become aware it is time to close your session with her. Trust yourself and the process. Deep work has been done. All is as it should.

• "Solar Plexus Chakra"

When a person exudes confidence, they have a presence that is palpable. The crystal, Orange Calcite, works to enable you to feel the confidence you so rightly deserve to feel. Take her and caress her silky body. The card is a tool. It sits before you as an example of energy in solid form. With the image of her in your mind, place Orange Calcite in the middle of your body, over your solar plexus chakra. She sits stationary atop you while you go inside and meditate about issues of massive proportions. Here, the elimination of trauma is addressed in a grand manner. Look away. I say it is so sad to comprehend that it is best to allow the angels to work with her so you may be spared images too coarse and ugly to imagine. Just rest. All is as it should be. Orange Calcite has taken her might and pulled out much related to gruesome war-related killings. There are many issues that surface around dismemberment, killing of children, rape, slavery, prostitution, and issues stemming from bullying. Pack them in a solar plexus and Orange Calcite wishes to see them removed.

    Stop after ten minutes of work. Allow the energy to settle. A day and a half is truly what is needed before using more crystals for healing. Water is needed to flush out impurities. When you feel absolutely strong and able to continue healing with crystals, begin again. The work is complete at this time. I see you enjoy working on yourself. You are brave.

Peridot

- ## "Solar Plexus Chakra"

Command. This is the word of the day. Command. If you take Peridot and ask her to do something, she will. Command and she bows at attention. The yearning to work with you is palatable. Reeking of cheer, she is here for you as a servant, guide, and healer—all trades related to releasing that which makes you buckle at the knees.

Take a moment and sit with your discomfort. Are you sure you want authority? Do you enjoy leaning on another for support. I believe you are ready to give up some dependency and demand authority.

Begin by placing Peridot near a window. The reflection of Light uniquely reflects onto its surface to create a film. This film, or screen, is helpful with transferring information to you. If you sit quietly while Peridot charges, listen to your inner voice. It screams and shouts what it wishes to clear with Peridot's assistance. Note the issues related to enslavement of character, power, and control.

You are now ready to do the healing work. Sit Peridot in your lap. She sits and weaves scores of information to your soul that cries for authority to be bestowed upon it. Cleared are enslavement traits and properties that elude the soul from knowing it is all powerful. The extraction of data basically permits new information to replace it. "Healthy and Happy" are conjoined to improve one's sense of self with respect to taking a stand. The work is fabulous, like a spider spinning a web. Fast, furious, fastidious, and fun.

Go take a bath after you are done. Ten minutes have gone by and you can now rest in the comfort of a tub of lukewarm water. Put in a few drops of lavender to clear your mind. This will allow the work done to settle. Make the bath water a bit tepid because no disruption is to come to the energy placed inside your solar plexus chakra. When you have performed this "bathing ritual" for about ten minutes, you are done. Say, "thank you," to Peridot. She enjoys this nicety.

- ## "Heart Chakra"

Peridot establishes itself as a crystal that marks time. I admire its wit and ability to take situations as they are fixed at a given moment and eliminate them from a time-space continuum. *Poof!* Vanish. The immediate transformation of character is apparent after Peridot has placed its intention on issues involving roaring rapids (Love's ups and downs). The tumult is what is fixed on and transmuted. You are left with a feeling so warm that you blissfully sit in a daze.

I suggest Peridot be placed in the center of your chest where your heart chakra resides beneath it. Patiently sit until you connect. Breathe and meditate. Find pleasure in knowing she has you to herself. No one can interfere at this moment. Peridot works beneath layers of skin. Deep concentration is necessary. Imagine you forge through layers of bobbing feelings. The ups and downs of heartache are gone as Peridot scoops it from the chakra center.

Drink water. Plenty of it. Now you are done. Five minutes is enough. Her work is powerful. When you reflect on the session, remind yourself you are exactly as you should be. The water ingested refreshes you during this reflection period. All is well.

Pink Tourmaline

- ## "Heart Chakra"

When a person is stress-ridden, take a heart-activated crystal and give it to them. A pink gem such as Pink Tourmaline calms, nourishes, and strengthens the soul. Find pleasure in giving this crystal to the one you adore. This soothes you, as well, during the time they are anxious.

What is interesting about using Pink Tourmaline is she holds you as long as you wish to be worked with. If you want more than actually what is written here, use your judgment to extend the time using her. There is no time limit to working with her. She is here to assist in the removal of all "heartfelt" problems. This includes drama with breakups, hurt feelings around betrayal, long silent treatments, divorce, and rabid sexual behavior—all drama and angst that create so much disturbance that people cannot understand why heartache is such a part of their everyday lives.

Within the structure of "Pink T," there is a structure within a structure, and so on… The more you delve, the more you realize she is plenty powerful. Each layer is built like a panel that provides nourishment. Each panel sits atop the next till it catapults down your heart chakra like dominoes spilling into a glass of milk.

Take a moment to sit and think about what you would like to address in a session with Pink T. She is ready when you intend what to release. Much is etherically relayed between the two of you as you consider what to work on. She hooks into your heart and you can feel her as a soft glow. To work in her

space is as gentle as holding a child who sleeps quietly in your arms. Please drink water during your "meeting" with Pink T. Your cells need replenishment as you journey to wellness.

Take a breath. Intend to remove aches and standing resentments. Imagine Pink T holds all the knowledge about what ails you. She takes layers, structured in DNA capsules, or compartments and shifts them, rocking them side to side. The motion is tremendous like shaking debris from a coal field. Each layer of debris is combed and layers are inspected. When the work is finished, silence falls upon you. How you end the session is your decision. She wants you to be completely satisfied with her work with you so do not hesitate to question whether there is more to be addressed.

How you know you are ready to rest is simple: Close one eye and focus. If it is blurry, you have eliminated much from your chakra. If the vision is clear, you may continue for a bit longer. Ten minutes is what we suggest for a full session with ten minutes added for more if needed.

Pyrite

- ## "Solar Plexus Chakra"

It is often a case of mistaken identity. The person holding Pyrite is confused. She has a quality that absorbs and muddles the senses. After she is in your hand, you awaken and realize Truth. Many find her trickery outstanding. They were lost and now they are found.

Pyrite crystal genuinely knows she is fooling you. She is respectful when she works in languages foreign to you. Often, she codes energies hiding her true nature so you see her as a friend and familiar cohort. When all is worked through, laces of energy stream out and leave like lost batons thrown out of stadiums in cheering competitions. The moment Pyrite escapes your grip, Heaven takes her and cleanses her. "In and out. Find me. I work on you. Try to catch me. Gone. Fool for attempting to know my ways..."

Rest a bit before holding her. Two hands, palms together with her in between them. Meditate and rest. Bring in warm energy as she trucks through your consciousness. Beaming into the solar plexus, she stands tall, making you feel so good, beautiful, light, and peaceful. Some find it a bit annoying, but the hum of a dishwasher seems to sound much like her working energy. There is a buzz... Can you hear it? Some feel a pulse when she extends herself to you.

This session can be used to treat wounds related to crime, war, passion and romance gone amuck—all issues where power turned on itself. Confusion is often a result of power plays gone wrong. Pyrite uses her wile to turn right side up what you turned upside down. Take a moment to consider how Pyrite assisted you.

After several minutes, relax. Pyrite can be put in a space where you feel her rays. Her good vibrations soften what is near.

Rest. Simple. Repeat. Drink water. Muscles need replenishment. This is good for today.

Red Jasper

- ## "Root Chakra"

Discussing root chakra issues is usually done in a format that is simplistic—easy to understand. The frame of reference by which I share my knowledge is fastened by years, lives, millennia of men who have soldiered through battles and won them. When I refer to soldier, I mean you—the soldier who carries a mission to learn how to free yourself from bonds that hold you and keep you down. When a man is free he can step forward. Red Jasper is the stone that enables each soldier to move towards Freedom's Gate.

Take Red Jasper, "RJ," and put her near the front of your skull where you might read a child's temperature. The forehead proves a good ground for scouting how to assess where you need attention. A "scope" goes into the membrane to see how RJ can work through layers to then delve in and eliminate fear. If you find that the work is very different from other stones you have used, you are correct. RJ has a passion that involves multiplicity. She works on levels that are profound and dense.

When you wake from your five minute session, you will find the issues that have surfaced are not how they had felt before. Longing for freedom from Mama and the desire to move—all issues involving hereditary and customary movement within a family system are now shifted in perspective. You can create a more positive outcome. When you relax in the notion you are free from existential angst and Mama and Papa are Love, where guilt is not apparent, you can better yourself in ways unheard of. The use of RJ moves you to get out and grow up. Please use her when the family is at your throat and more can be achieved if you leave what no longer serves you.

- ## "Sacral Chakra"

If you would like to address issues that interfere with your ability to manifest, please sit and listen. I suggest you use Red Jasper to remove energy that causes negativity where events you plan do not come to be. Fruition is the operative word. If you have not been fruitful, you need to adjust the energy so all can stream out from within you and stream in from outside you. This balance is necessary to produce marvelous creations.

Red Jasper has properties unlike others. Some stones are set apart in appearance to cause a distinct reaction for the one holding it. If you hold a piece of Red Jasper, many will say feelings of comfort, wisdom, and peace emanate from it.

I wish to note that working around sacral chakra issues is very important. When you delve inside this arena, much is revealed. Take a few breaths. Cleanse the temple that is your body by breathing in Love to your core. Inhale and then exhale waste. It is important to rid the body of energy that lowers your vibration. Deep breathing assists in preparing you for the work to be done here. With your right hand on the stone, take a moment to concentrate on what you wish to release. Any time you feel stagnant, the sacral chakra is being challenged. Moments of "why do I never see the end result?" or "how could this be so difficult to perform and see through to completion?" are just two examples of what can be addressed for release. Eye your prize, meaning visualize what you wish to achieve. The moment there is a connection between your issue or problem and the end result you wish to achieve, you will feel a rush. This whoosh is just how Red Jasper works. Immediate results. Extract negativity and replace with what needs to be addressed in order to grow and become a working, participating member of the Universe.

You will feel tired after she has done her job. True. Rest. Relax. Feet up. Enjoy simple pleasure. Eat as you would normally. Take time to consider how you have grown during this exercise. It is a pleasure having her in your grace. She enjoys a simple acknowledgement for the effort she put towards your growth. She is humble and kind. A friend. Enjoy this moment as she bonded with you in order for you to know how to be a better friend to yourself.

Rose Quartz

- "Heart Chakra"

Women fashion jewelry with Rose Quartz. The statement is simply Love. This warm romance of a specimen is redeemed through all time and space. Include this crystal in a necklace or ornament when you want to invoke beauty. Rose Quartz's beauty pulls up what is to shine brightly that is first and foremost in one's heart. Men enjoy "Rosie," too. She shines for them so they may heal wounds on many levels.

Take her and hold her all by herself. She gleans magic as you work independently with her. "Love is the answer," she cries loudly for all to hear. When you see that you release much with her assistance, you will feel that the work you do is private and intimate. She prefers solitude, so remain seated where others are not near you. Rosie likes balance and private places enable her to feel this way.

Consider how you wish to heal using her power of Love. Take three breaths. Touch the stone to your heart, invoking God Almighty to be present during this session. Much Love streams through you. Now, imagine caves. The caves worm their way through openings (in your heart chakra) until they hit center. Each cave is situated solely to assist in Love-related matters. The cleansing is pure and simple. Each pulse of Light that she shines connects to an entrance, cleansing it the way a portal is cleansed. You feel something, yet it is imperceptible to

the touch. On a cellular level, this is distributed evenly through the chakra. When you are still, she moves quickly, calmly making entrances clear for more Love to filter in. If you tire, stop. Your work has been done.

    If you have the energy to continue, sit and listen for the moment when she tires. No energy in her body will be felt for your remedying this chakra. Put the card in a place where light shines on her, preferably a window that is filled with sunshine. "Wash" the card with Love by placing the intention that she is clear of energies that diffuse her power. This cleansing can take several minutes.

    In about one hour, she is free and may be stacked with the deck—her close friends. Immediately after using Rosie, rest, nap, sip tea or water. Do nothing but sit. I recommend a bath, too, if you feel toxic and wish to enjoy clearing all that has risen to be released. Thank her and refresh yourself with a good night's sleep.

Ruby

- "Root Chakra"

"I charm the pants off you," she says to those who are with her. Ruby is a gentle, happy child who is frequently kissed by strangers. In the hands of Love, she whispers, "I'm here. Trust this is good. We work together to enable you to move and then run!" Ruby is a beauty. She can quickly assess strength, combat weakness, determine whether Light can be brought in for healing, and offer advice—all at once.

Let's discuss her properties. She is smooth and silky in all ways and she drifts through time well. Other crystals have more stagnant energy and are less able to move from place to place. Ruby is a drifter. She sinks in, devours what is to be returned to Heaven, and comes out singing happily. Ruby needs sun, so please spend time placing her in hot spots when possible. Ruby is unique in that she sings. She is a troubadour in that her high notes go deep. She is very reverent to Mary Magdalene and resonates with her energy.

The work to be done is this: Place two feet together. Sit in a chair, resting your face in your hands. Ruby is to be on your lap. Imagine she is a doll. Instruct her to use her wile and remove pain that keeps you from being free in all ways. The minute you begin, sit back and allow her to be a child, singing through

the root chakra. All issues around loneliness, isolation, and abandonment are reviewed. She makes decisions about what is to be released. Karma is addressed. You are invited here to imagine all issues are uncovered where you can now live in harmony and peace. Good. Sip water. It makes for smooth passage with healing when you do this.

Tears may flow. Your spirit allows great healing if you cry. Please rest after working so closely with Ruby. She needs time to adjust after her session, too. Keep her from the other crystals for a day; it is important to give her space while she returns to herself again, rejuvenated and bright.

Take time to walk and listen to the words in your head. It is here now that lessons are learned. The session is complete and you have journeyed well. Thank Ruby for her gift of healing. She appreciates the Love and receives it happily.

Sandstone

• "Third-Eye Chakra"

This beaut has a chemistry that eats through issues in the blink of an eye. "Sandy" has a strong desire to go through layers that are unjust, unfair—they do not fill the needs of the soul. Issues are cleansed and removed with her assistance.

Lie on your side, preferably the right side. Hold Sandy in your hand with her picture facing your palm. Rest. Imagine that issues of war and insanity are removed. All issues involving rape are also addressed and released.

This crystal kicks up issues as it works. You may cry or shiver. Release all involving shame, guilt, and longing for Love. Trust this is going to be very effective in shifting your behaviors, specifically romantic and sexual.

By the time you are done (five to ten minutes), you will have removed a lot of misery from your third eye. This "knowing" comes from clarity—overall clear thought, sight, and hearing that what you experience is Truth.

Find time to meditate. See if this is possible. The more you can find time to rest, the better you are at being still and able to get through challenges that life offers. Thank you for trusting Sandy. Please "wash" her by setting her in light, preferably moonlight. If sun is what you desire, a card left for hours in daylight heals and re-energizes her, as well.

Sapphire

- ## "Throat Chakra"

"Beam me up!" she declares. Sapphire uses rays of Light to repair throat chakra "ailments." She takes many lessons from consciousnesses in galaxies far from Earth. Sapphire transmutes negative energies in a cosmic fashion. Bull's eye! Right on the mark! She uses technologies that are advanced in order to address what you would call illnesses of the throat.

Place her directly on your throat chakra. She needs to be positioned in the center of your larynx. Give her a moment to sit with the energy that is in your body. She calibrates to find exactly how to transmit energy to you. Be patient. A few minutes of reflection while she hooks up with you is enough time.

Sit and quietly hum. Vibration enacts healing. Vibration serves as a catalyst to release pain. Sapphire grabs it, disintegrating all in a steady motion. Like waves, she takes particles and turns them over until they are gone. Light is replaced as a healing medicine where pain, tears, longing, suffering, greed, and avarice existed. The process is painful; you might cry. Part of your journey is to suffer in order to free yourself of all encumbrances. When pain is eliminated, you are free.

The work is complete when you feel tired. If you do not, the time spent on the throat should take approximately ten minutes. Lift Sapphire from your body. Place her in a window. Light heals and replenishes her. Thank her and enjoy your new you.

- ## "Third-Eye Chakra"

Precious as a Ruby, Emerald, or Diamond, Sapphire poses as a sacred, trusted friend among her peers. In time, she melts into you the way a gem seeds its information through layers, or membranes to your soul. "For all I've done for you, I wish you peace, dear friend," she shares. This is her mantra. Peace is her desire. She gently works through layers, combing as she toils, in order to break through mire you have accumulated over eons of lifetimes.

Take Sapphire and place her between your hands. Hold her as you lift them towards your face over your third-eye chakra. Breathe, letting out steam—the anger you hold in your eye. This process takes a few minutes. Breathe. Let the information she emits go deep inside as you work with her. Deep breaths allow her to go in your chakra, working through "forbidden zones." These areas are hidden; you allow her to go inside and clear what you have hidden from yourself.

The work is complete when you feel peace. A sense of relief is experienced. You rest. Take her and place her in the sun. She requires replenishment. Thank her and continue on with your day.

Selenite

- **"Third-Eye Chakra"**

The object of desire... This crystal is so powerful that angels encrypt messages with it. It acts like a radar, beacon, wand, deflector, magnet, trophy, and skewer—it enables one to affix multiple energies on it when removing negativity from another. If you are in a bind, please use this tool with caution. It is extremely important to know how powerful it is. Do not treat Selenite as if it were any ol' object. Make sure you know its capabilities before working with it. So many individuals treat her as if she were a toy.

When you begin working with Selenite, hold her in your hand with palms up. Show her in your own way that she is special. Perhaps a remark or gesture will convey your respect. You begin. She targets third-eye issues very rapidly and multi-tasks well. She removes old energies that prevent your moving forward. If sadness, health issues, drama, old lifestyle habits, or laziness have you upset, she will have fun telling this chakra where to go. Place her in your dominant hand. Pass her over your third eye. One pass is all that is needed. She calms the area and removes betrayal, as well as other issues that diminish your well-being. Imagine many issues envelop your soul and are being addressed quickly. They are swiftly removed. When your soul is ready to release issues that no longer serve you, you feel relief. A sense of calm comes over you. You are to put Selenite near a window. The cleansing of light recharges her. Complete, you rest. Drink water today. This removes particles of energy that stream to your physical vessel. Good job. Thank her and bid her a good night.

• "Crown Chakra"

You can place Selenite over your head as if she were a cap. The cap is very heavy; it carries much energy in it. If you work with her as a clearer of energies that block your connection to others, please be careful. Her weight is dense and powerful. Sit still during this exercise. No need to fear. Remove all expectations, sit, and allow yourself to fill with Love as she removes unwanted energies that distance you from All That Is.

Take a moment to sit. Just sit. All is as it should be. Remove clothes that are tight, specifically near your head. If you have a jacket on, please move the sleeves so they are long and to your wrists (no bunching). It is a process to clear the mind, so the body is to be carefully inspected and treated as if it were a jewel, too. When your mind and body are clear of any intrusions and discomforts, place Selenite atop your crown. Balance is necessary. If you cannot, put on a hat. Please be patient, for this process might feel a bit arduous.

Rely on your mind to guide you. With eyes closed, take time to imagine you are walking. Then sit down. Find a field with flowers. Place a flower in your hair. The colors erupt. You are wild with Light. (Selenite is clearing you now.) You are in a meadow and the flower in your hair radiates, pulses energy. You are ablaze. Remove all inhibitions. Go deep inside and count from 10 to 1. You are now complete and healing has occurred. Step from your meadow and return to your home here. When you have settled into your current space, drink water.

Selenite removes obstacles hindering you from finding peace and connection with Spirit. You relax and find comfort in this exercise, knowing that all is as it should be. Selenite, the crystal of old, is happy to return you to your self that knows this is so.

Silver

- ## "Root Chakra"

Silver is unique in that the property inside amasses energy to such proportions that you gasp at the sight of it. Particles of Light distribute themselves in a maze-like structure to band the energy together for massive, influential healing on a grand scale. Peer inside this matrix. See how beautiful the latticework is. It holds much Love for you. Enjoy this healing.

Place Silver along your arm or leg for a short time. A minute is needed. It aligns with the root when touching your limb. Next, place it near your pelvis, down at your crotch. Hold on to her while you sit and breathe a few times, relaxing with each exhale. Now you are ready.

Imagine a gym. There are barbells, weights, mats, and machines. You are in a structure that is very powerful. Much work is done in this place. Silver is the gym and you have placed yourself in her care. She takes energy and aligns it so you have a framework where trust and safety are addressed. Mapped out

are perceptions to adjust and events to review why you flee when things go poorly. All your work is internal. Hold Silver; she works in the bowels, the recesses of your existence so you may charge confidently onward.

This work is complete when you feel comfort in knowing there was work done for your benefit. It is a subtle, yet gnawing feeling that all is as it should and you can leave her for today. Remove her from your body. Place a hand on your pelvis and repeat, "All is well. This is done." She provides solace while you repeat this phrase. Thank her. She enjoys the gratitude you share.

Smokey Quartz

- "Root Chakra"

Evidenced by her stature is a unique mix of oil. The deposits in her frame are magical. "Smokey Q" is a dreamy, "let's be friends and play in the Universe" type of friend. Crystals have certain personalities. She is adventurous and romantic. She prefers solitude, which is counterintuitive to play and romance. The dreamer insists on being alone in her happy adventure. When you join her for talk and more, it livens her. When you leave, she is content to remain by herself.

Smokey Q has a story: She had a reservoir of energy and put it in a jar. Many individuals took her energy, using it for practices that were prohibited by officials of The Council of Light. She remained true and steadfast by allowing others to use her, yet her pained frame finally puttered out. Many journeyed to find cause for the malady. She was injected with images of consolation to pull her through the darkness. Now, she resonates with high energy souls, refusing to be toyed with and used for malice. She has the ability to refuse work if it is not commanded for the betterment of others.

Place her in a section of the room for privacy and solitude. Pray for good tidings and a healthy outcome for your healing session. Remove clothing with zippers or buckles. All metal is to be taken off. Drink water to infuse you with a high concentration of energy. This is necessary to ensure a wonderful, successful experience with her.

Smokey Q can sit on your pelvis. Trust she works well in this pose, like a statue in a park. Rest. She adjusts to your stature and remains steady as she calibrates exactly how to remove debris from your root chakra. War, enemies, fields of dead and dying—images that haunt you—are removed. Fields or meadows with daisies and birds are substituted for these bombed-out landscapes. All issues related to "Love under fire" where you may have been pressured to make choices about mates are reviewed and considered for removal. In a short time, five to ten minutes, the work is complete.

Drink water. Rest. Consume energy drinks if need be: juice of all kinds, water with lemon. Now you are done. Take Smokey Q and place her near a vent or chimney. Any shaft will do. The air will suck out the dark energy she absorbed. She likes this manner of cleansing. Go to the bathroom and eliminate. This will achieve better results. Thank you for working so diligently. The rewards are great.

Sodalite

- "Third-Eye Chakra"

Her energy is soft. She is no longer brazen. Sodalite fashions herself in bracelets, earrings, and pendants, all for the sake of beauty. Can we see past "Glam Girl?" There was a period of time between when she was coarse and when she became soft. Sodalite turned around. She has a story to tell:

"I left home when I was..." (Ah! She has a sense of humor!) "It began ages of ages ago... Mystics speak of blue patterns in time. I was called, as they beckoned me to assist. It is around this time when bells were used for healing. I came to be a special 'magnet' of sorts for those who wanted comfort. Disillusionment and pain disappeared, but there were still those who held bitterness. They demanded I work as a slave for the removal of all ills. I became embittered. After lives, or songs, as I like to say, I realized the bitterness I carried hurt not only me, but also the ones needing my Light. Change was necessary. Peace ensued. I am now a channel of peace and harmony. Today, I am true to myself and swayed by no one. Thank you."

The message we received is that crystals have energies and there are some who abuse the privilege to work with these Light-minded energies. Sodalite assists you as a servant in healing ills that are in the recesses of your third-eye chakra. Take her and work gently over the spot across your brow. If you need assistance, ask her to guide you as to which direction she prefers to be "swiped" across your forehead. Take two or three breaths and then imagine she works diligently in a crisscross fashion, weaving in energy. Your hand holds her as she weaves across, down, and back again. This ensues for approximately ten to fifteen minutes. Despite this fairly long process, you eliminate "chakra fatigue." This is overstress to the area. Many lifetimes of sadness are reviewed and considered for release.

After your healing, lay her down gently. She rests. Thank her for patiently weaving Light, removing debris, and connecting with you on a deep soul level. Drink water to hydrate yourself. All is well.

Tiger's Eye

- **"Sacral Chakra"**

Trust the energy as it enters you. Tiger's Eye is very versed in being able to transport its energy to places that are wounded. Take a moment to clear your body. Speak softly to yourself, reminding you that all is as it should be. Close your mind. Go inside and dream that you are having angels clear away debris. When you feel you are in a calm space, begin the work. Tiger's Eye is ready to address how you came to be sad and discouraged around issues of fame, popularity, affluence, and abundance.

    First, lift your legs. Have them raised upon a table, desk, or chair. Doing this makes for a more effective clearing. Place Tiger's Eye over your sacral chakra, below your belly button. Let her pulse. She removes incorrigible behavior from lifetimes ago. If you cry, this is understandable. Issues surface and emotions are expelled. Hold her in your hand while she works with you. The energy is strong and you will bond with her. After a few minutes, please remove her from your body. Place her in an area where light will rest upon her visage. Sunlight is fantastic; moonlight is superb. You sleep after this healing work. Dream of what has transpired. She is in your thoughts.

• "Solar Plexus Chakra"

This stone is valuable. It is part of a dyad. The property involves salt—common salt found in various parts of the earth. The salt in the stone gives it an iridescent quality that draws the eye to it. Thank Salt for its cooperation. The shimmer is how Tiger's Eye operates. Blind Love—it will work for anyone and anything without question. Its nature is unconditional.

Take about a tablespoon of salt and rub it on your belly (Authors' note: Himalayan salt or sea salt). Remove any excess salt. This creates a wonderful staging platform for the work to be done. Tiger's Eye is to be placed directly on the solar plexus, which is located under the rib cage in the center of your torso. Take a breath and hold it for a few seconds. Remove the stone and allow the healing to occur. You have left the stones's energy imprint on your body. It works furiously to remove suffering billowed up regarding war. Hate and greed are also addressed. Forgiveness work is done etherically. Place your intention on ridding yourself of old habits involving contentious behavior and belittlement. When the work is complete, you may feel sad. Much is exposed. Guilt and shame surface. Take time to rest. The aura has been cleansed and you may retire to sleep. It is a very powerful session that can make you sleepy. Drink water. Find yourself dreaming about what has occurred. Thank Tiger's Eye for the Love it gave you and how it exposed and eliminated what you did not wish to carry in your soul.

Topaz

- **"Solar Plexus Chakra"**

She shines like a Diamond. What a beautiful crystal. I see you wondering why Diamond was mentioned. Topaz has qualities that are similar to Diamond in that they inherit qualities of beauty, brilliance, brains, and brawn. Both are chosen to work on issues around seeing yourself as a magnificent being of Love. When powerful objects are incorporated into your structure (body) for healing purposes, monumental change occurs.

Topaz longs to remove objects that throw you from center. The solar plexus is a good starting point. When you touch her, imagine she says, "Hello," to you. She immediately incorporates her energy into your body. Take a moment to sit and bond as she gets to know you. Then, gently place her over your solar plexus. She does not like swift movements. They are called "rude awakenings" to her. Breathe in and out. Release wounds that stifle you. Topaz works inside this chakra as you breathe. She is fond of the work you do using

intention. When you actively work with her, she radiates. The pulse is strong. Go deeper inside, removing layers of pain that bother you. As you imagine you are releasing issues, she continues along with her work. Much headway is made working in tandem.

Remove Topaz from your body after about ten minutes. Place her in a heated environment where there is activity. If no area of this sort can be found, imagine she is doused with pure heat, Love, and a lot of buzzy energy. Rest and drink water, for you have accomplished a lot with her today.

Turquoise

- **"Throat Chakra"**

Native Americans revere this stone that calls up images of animals and winds and fire. If you hear messages from her, believe they breathe Truth from the ages. The mighty oak stands tall. Turquoise also stands erect during her sessions. Without her strength, many tribes could not have defeated drought and famine. Survival with the sacred gem—this is what the natives believed so fiercely. In turn, Turquoise is beholden to the people. She reveres man and wishes a time comes when all unite in Love.

Take a palm and rest Turquoise flat down with her face in your hand (picture of stone facing your palm). Remove debris in your aura by waving this palm in the air around your body. If you are unable to balance the card, hold it between your fingertips and wave it to clear your aura. This takes a minute. Now, put her gently on your throat. If she slips, hold her. Again, have her face your body. Remember to breathe. Use her energy to recall times when you spoke quietly

and did not assert yourself effectively. Use this time to release blocks that caused you to stifle yourself and go silent. These and other issues around complacency, docility, and gripping fear that left you speechless are addressed.

When you have cleared these issues from your throat, imagine placing them where they are no longer able to bother you. You can imagine that a sphere holds them and carries them to Spirit or you can radiate energy that removes them from your mind altogether. However you choose, the work is done and there is now more free space to create genuine loud and clear speech. Your heart is full, knowing issues are gone and you have turned a corner. Turquoise is tremendously pleased with your healing work. Together, you created much Light.

We hope you enjoyed working with Carry Me Crystals as much as we enjoyed co-creating this for you.